GW00360018

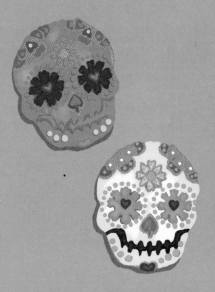

TACOS

Lily Ramirez-Foran

CONTENTS

INTRODUCTION

A GIRL AND HER GOAT

'Chivo brincado, chivo quedado' is an old Mexican saying that literally means 'a skipped goat is a left goat'. It foretells the fate of a woman, referred to as a goat in the saying (don't even get me started on that one!), who is skipped in the marrying order. If your younger sister gets married before you, you are most likely going to be left on the shelf to rot. Not very nice, right? Well, my friends, that was supposed to be my fate: I was a skipped goat. Growing up in Mexico, marriage was pretty much the one and only thing a young lady like me could and should aspire to in my family's eyes. This goat, however, had other plans.

I was always a bit different: too opinionated, too feisty, too outspoken, too ambitious, too smart – I was too many 'toos' for my own good. On the eve of my little sister's wedding, a nosy aunt was sympathising with me over my 'skipped goat' situation and I got so angry, I told her I would make tacos of the bloody goat and sell them if I needed to!

When I finally did get married, the family breathed a sigh of relief. Another aunt went so far as to thank my husband, Alan, on our wedding day for marrying me. I laugh about it now, but I wasn't amused back then. Having said that, though, I must have had my doubts at some point because I found a recipe for goat meat tacos tucked away in the last few notes of my diary before I left Mexico for Ireland.

When I started writing this, I found myself thinking it was quite fitting that my first book should be about tacos. When my friend and publisher, Kristin Jensen, reached out back in January 2021 with her idea for the Blasta Books series, I was on board instantly. After chatting for only a few minutes, the idea of a small but mighty book on tacos came up and instead of shying away from the crazy idea of narrowing down almost four millennia of taco recipes into a baker's dozen (like any other self-respecting Mexican would do), I relished the challenge.

The only logic behind the recipes that I chose is that these are my favourite tacos and toppings right now. They are recipes that I cook all the time at home or at my shop, Picado, without the need for specialised equipment. These are also recipes that have some relevance to my life in Ireland, my greatest hits of 2021. And my fellow Mexicans (and possibly every Aztec god out there), please spare me the angry litany of omissions that I can already hear: but what about tacos de canasta, tacos de carnitas, tacos de birria, tacos governador? The book is only 65 pages long, and besides, I need some material left over for my epic Hollywood-movie-ready book on the girl who had a goat and made some tasty tacos.

So here it is, a small book on tacos, as no goat should be left behind and tacos were, after all, the very first thing I cooked on my own here in Ireland. May you find plenty of fun and tasty ideas to turn your goat (or whatever other meat or veggie rocks your boat) into something delicious to eat.

TACOS RULE

Tacos are quintessential to Mexican cuisine. In a country of stark contrasts, with huge economic and social divides, tacos transcend. They know no boundaries of class or creed – everybody eats them and you'll find them everywhere from a humble shack on the side of the road to a Michelin three-star restaurant. Great tacos feature in the lives of Mexican people every day. If you ever find yourself in Mexico, you can be sure of one thing: in Mexico, tacos are king.

Let me start by clarifying a crucial point: tortillas are not the same as tacos, just as bread is not the same as a sandwich. You need tortillas for tacos as much as you need bread for a sandwich, but a tortilla does not become a taco until you fill it with something. Without a filling, you just have two pieces of bread, right? So please don't go searching for 'tacos' in the shops when what you really want are tortillas to make tacos with.

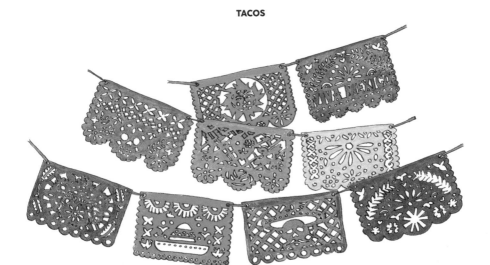

Also, there is a HUGE difference between a tortilla and a wrap. A Mexican tortilla is made out of corn. With a rich history going back 9,000 years, corn is beloved in Mexico. As a nation, we eat approximately 600,000 tons of corn tortillas every day – they are the staple of our diet. So when we talk about tortillas, we are always referring to those made out of 100% corn.

When the first ships of Spanish conquistadores arrived on Mexican shores in the early 1500s, they brought wheat with them. They considered the native corn crop dirty and impure and wouldn't eat it. Wheat was a clear status symbol and corn was left for the plebs. The early crops of wheat, however, weren't great and making bread proved to be very difficult.

Early Portuguese Jews arriving from Spain followed the conquistadores to the New World and settled in the arid territories of the north-west of the country in what we know now as the estates of Chihuahua and Sonora, where they sowed wheat to make matzah, their traditional unleavened Passover bread. What came out of these early trials resembled the round, flat discs that Mexicans called tortillas.

Fast forward a few hundred years and you find perfected wheat tortillas or wraps – lovely and delicious, but with no true relation to Mexican corn tortillas. Don't get me wrong, you can make perfectly good tacos with wheat wraps, but they are different from proper corn tortillas.

WHAT MAKES A GREAT TACO?

I once read that tacos were an infinite universe with endless possibilities. It makes sense – there are literally thousands of taco recipes in Mexico. Every region has its own repertoire and discovering Mexico through its tacos makes for an incredibly delicious life-long journey.

A taco can be made of basically anything that you can eat wrapped in a tortilla. With so many choices, nailing down what makes a taco great is a difficult job. Is it a particular filling? A specific topping? Is it down to the salsa that crowns the taco? Or maybe it goes beyond the physical. Perhaps it's the memory of a moment of delight when biting into a warm, soft, fluffy corn tortilla wrapped around tender slow-cooked meat and topped with a tangy, fiery, homemade salsa. Is it the company? Is it the place? The many elements and layers of a taco make the idea of the ultimate taco pretty unattainable, and yet, stubborn as I am, I persist.

I've dedicated a ridiculous amount of time to thinking about what makes a taco great. I've studied the masters, read all the literature and come to the conclusion that whatever rocks your boat makes a good taco as long as you have the following components:

- An excellent corn tortilla, warmed with a few brown spots

- A tender and flavoursome filling (whether it's meat or veggies)

- Some fresh toppings that achieve the right balance between creaminess and crunchiness because texture is important (raw onion, fresh coriander, lime, shredded cabbage, a drizzle of cream, cheese, peanuts, crispy chicken or pork skins, etc.)

- A hint of acidity (lime, pickles, pineapple, hot sauce, vinegar, etc.)

- A salsa to crown it all (because the right level of heat is paramount and a dry taco is no taco at all).

Next time you're thinking of free-styling your tacos, remember these elements and play around with the infinite options. Once you have at least one of each of the above, your taco should be perfect! Don't be afraid to experiment. Some of the non-traditional recipes in this book came out of playful (and sometimes frustrating) days in the kitchen. You'll win some and lose some, but that's what makes cooking so much fun.

Carne asada tacos

MASTERING THE ART OF
HOLDING A TACO

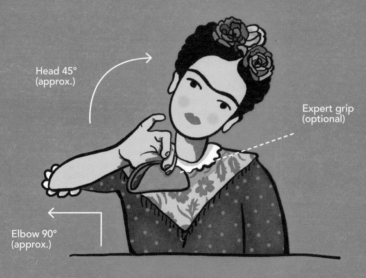

Head 45°
(approx.)

Expert grip
(optional)

Elbow 90°
(approx.)

Plate ALWAYS
under the taco

The pleasure of filling a warm corn tortilla with something delicious and eating it with your hands, perfectly balanced without any awkwardness, is hard to describe. The art of holding a taco properly is almost instinctive for a Mexican, who will always bring the taco towards their mouth while simultaneously bowing to the taco because the taco is king. But if you don't have it in your DNA, it's a matter of delicious practice – the more tacos you eat, the better you get at it. But a good, sturdy tortilla will help you fake it until you make it as a Mexican.

EXPERT TIP: If men eat tacos while wearing a suit and tie, they tend to flip the tie over their shoulder to avoid any spills.

CORN TORTILLAS

SERVES 4–6

The first time I made corn tortillas in Ireland by hand, I made a mess of it. I used up my next monthly phone call home to talk to my mam about it. My family are third-generation traditional tortilla bakers, so not getting my tortillas right was a stain on the family's name that I couldn't bear! My mam's advice was to forget everything I knew and remember what Grandpa Pedro said: 'Masa is alive.' To this day, I share that same advice with our students in the cookery school.

Practice makes perfect, so give it a few goes and don't be discouraged by mistakes. The recipe is very simple, but it looks long because I'm sharing as many tips as I can to give you confidence and to explain the method in detail, helping you avoid the mistakes I made myself.

500ml boiling water

300g Mexican masa harina

¹/₈ tsp table salt

MAKING THE TORTILLAS

Heat a dry, non-stick crêpe or pancake pan over a medium-high heat for 5 minutes. While the pan heats, boil the kettle with about 600ml of water (it's good to have a little extra in addition to the 500ml called for in the recipe in case the dough needs it).

❶ Put the masa harina and salt in a large heatproof bowl and mix it well using a fork. Pour the 500ml of boiling water over the dry ingredients and start mixing everything with your fork. Use your fork as if you were mashing potatoes with it, pressing with the back of the tines to bring everything together to form a dough. Don't stick your hands into the dough until you're absolutely sure you won't burn yourself. Masa sticks to your fingers like caramel and it can cause serious burns if you're not careful.

❷ As soon as you can work with the dough without getting burned, ditch the fork and bring it all together with your hands. Your aim is to form one big ball of warm masa with the consistency of wet playdough. You do not need to knead the masa for a certain amount of time or rest it because there is no gluten in corn, so there are no gluten strands to develop. As soon as it comes together in a smooth ball, the masa is ready.

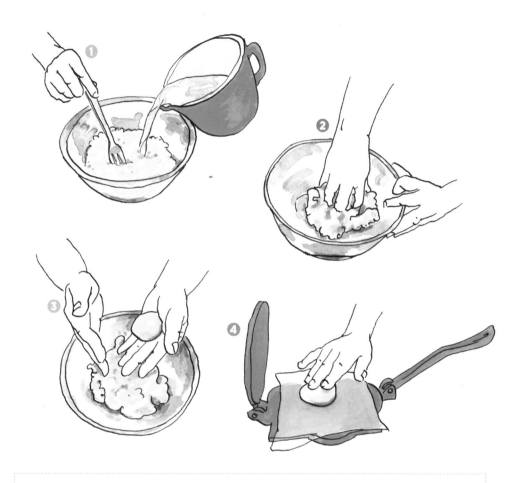

DIY TORTILLA PRESS

If you want to get serious about making tortillas, a tortilla press is imperative. However, don't get one for your very first time – make them as outlined in this recipe, then if you love them, buy a cast iron tortilla press (don't bother with plastic or aluminium ones, they're no good). If you don't have a tortilla press, use two heavy wooden boards and apply pressure with your body until you have a thin tortilla. Make sure you press the masa between two pieces of plastic, otherwise you won't be able to peel the tortilla off the wood.

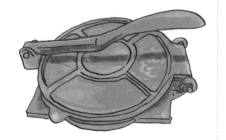

Because masa is quite sticky, it must be pressed between two sheets of plastic or else it will stick to the cast iron press. Open your tortilla press and line it with one of the plastic sheets that comes with it (no single-use plastic here!). Use those sheets till they are in tatters, then replace them with a freezer bag cut into two, which is the best plastic for the job.

3 Roll some masa between your palms to make a ball slightly smaller than the size of a golf ball (around 30g). Place it in the middle of the tortilla press, on top of the plastic sheet, bang on in the centre. Tortilla presses have a design fault – the pressure is greater closer to the handle – so placing your ball exactly in the centre will give you a more even tortilla. If it does go off centre, the tortilla will spill outside of the edges of the press and break.

4 Press the ball of masa slightly with your fingers to prevent it from rolling out of place. Cover the ball with the second piece of plastic. **5** Close the lid of the tortilla press and press it using the handle. **6** Open the tortilla press again and you'll see that your ball of dough is now a perfectly round and evenly thin tortilla – it should be slightly thicker than a sheet of paper. If it's too thick, though, close the tortilla press and put a little more pressure in the handle this time. You'll get the hang of this pretty quickly.

7 Peel off the top plastic sheet. Lift the second plastic sheet (which now has the tortilla on it) and flip it into your hand, leaving the tortilla resting in your hand and peeling off the plastic easily that way.

Resist the temptation to make loads of little balls, press them all and then cook them together. For masa to work, it must be wet and hot. The minute the masa starts cooling off or drying out your tortillas will suffer, so keep the masa in one big ball for as long as possible and make just one tortilla at a time. You'll get so good at making them, you won't even notice.

COOKING THE TORTILLAS

Tortillas have a soft side and a hard side and we give these to them through the way we cook them. This is ancient knowledge, so pay attention to it, as the success of your tortilla depends on it.

8 Place the tortilla in the completely dry preheated pan – no butter, oil or grease in any shape or form – and cook it for 10 seconds. The tortilla should now glide around on the pan, so using your fingers, slide it towards you and flip it gently. Cook the second side of the tortilla for 1 minute.

As soon as the 1 minute timer goes off, use an egg lifter or fish slice to flip the tortilla again to finish cooking the first side. At this point, your tortilla should slowly start to rise in a gorgeous puff. Do not touch it until it stops puffing or it collapses, at which point it is fully cooked and ready to be taken out of the pan and into your tortilla cosy or tea towel (see pages 12–13 on heating your tortillas).

Cooking the tortillas this way gives them their structure, creating a soft side (the one that you cooked in two parts) and a hard side (the side that was cooked for 1 minute). The structure of your tortilla is very important, as if you cook both sides for too long, you'll have two hard sides, which means the tortilla will have no flexibility and it will crack when you try to roll it or fold it. On the other hand, if you don't cook it long enough on both sides, the tortilla will be too soft and it will fall apart when you try to fill it. The hard side is always used as the outside of the taco to give the taco more robustness, while the soft side is the one that cradles the filling and absorbs some of the juices.

Repeat all the steps above until you have used up all the masa. Halfway through the dough, you might notice that the tortilla edges start getting jagged – this is a sign that your masa has dried. Just top it up with a little bit of lukewarm water from the kettle and knead it again to refresh it. The tortilla edges will be smooth again.

9 Take the tortilla out of the pan (with an egg lifter or fish slice so you don't burn yourself from the steam) and place it into your cosy or tea towel with the soft side facing down. This will prevent them from sticking to each other. Fresh tortillas last two or three days max, so it's best to make only what you need. Store any leftovers wrapped in a clean tea towel inside a plastic bag in the fridge.

TO HEAT
OR NOT TO HEAT?
THAT IS NOT EVEN A QUESTION!

When I first arrived in Ireland 20 years ago, I couldn't find Mexican tortillas to save my life. The bagel craze was dying down and wraps were starting to make an appearance. I walked into a chain of sandwich bars and got overly excited when I saw a wrap on the menu. I didn't care that it wasn't corn, I just wanted one. But when it arrived, it was cold. My face dropped and rage took over, which is not difficult when you have a fiery Latin temper like mine. What do you mean, you're giving me a cold wheat tortilla? What do you mean, they don't need to be heated? I almost self-combusted! So a big hint here: whether it's a corn or a wheat tortilla, Mexicans always heat them.

Heating is imperative when it comes to corn — corn doesn't have any gluten, so it has zero elasticity when it's cold. In the early days of selling corn tortillas in Ireland, the number one complaint I would get from customers was about tortillas breaking. It took some prodding to realise they were attempting to use them cold, pretty much like they'd use wheat wraps. I'm telling you, you ain't ever gonna fold a cold corn tortilla. It will always break.

Mexicans heat corn tortillas on a comal, which is a flat skillet heated up to a high heat. In Ireland, I quickly found that a non-stick crêpe or pancake pan or even a regular non-stick frying pan works perfectly well. The secret is to have it at the right heat. If you don't preheat your pan, the tortillas — whether they're homemade or shop bought — will stick.

Heat your tortillas by putting a dry, non-stick frying pan over a high heat for about 5 minutes. After the 5 minutes are up, lower the heat to medium-high, place a corn tortilla in the pan and heat it for 40 seconds on each side, until the tortilla is soft and pliable, before removing it from the pan. I keep my tortillas warm in a tortilla cosy (we sell them at Picado), but you can also wrap them in a thick, clean tea towel with some tin foil on the outside to keep them warm until you need to use them.

CAN YOU HEAT TORTILLAS IN A MICROWAVE?

This brings me nicely to one of the questions I get asked most often: can you heat corn tortillas in the microwave? My Mexican mama would say feck no, but after years of cooking for a crowd in Ireland with just one crêpe pan (as opposed to a comal that's so big it stretches across four rings on the hob), I say feck yes, because you've got to be realistic! Still, you should use a microwave only if you have a tortilla cosy or are absolutely desperate. Never heat your tortillas for more than 1 minute at the beginning, and then, if they're not perfect, at 30-second intervals at a time thereafter. The more tortillas you are heating in one go, the more 30-second intervals you'll need.

The microwave messes with the moisture content of tortillas and corn doesn't like it. More often than not, you'll end up with limp tortillas that are overly soft or too steamy to give any sort of structure to your taco. Remember, the tortilla is the cradle of the taco and no one enjoys a taco that falls apart on the first bite. So while a cosy does help, the microwave is not a perfect solution, no matter what the internet tells you. Mark my words, you're better off heating them one at a time on a pan, as they will have a better texture and hence you will have a better taco.

A RECIPE IS NOTHING WITHOUT ITS CONTEXT

I have backed myself into a corner when it comes to Mexican food. All those years complaining about fake Mexican food and Tex-Mex or Cali-Mex food passing as Mexican have turned me into a purist. If I had a penny for every time I've had to tell someone that chilli con carne isn't a Mexican dish, I would be rich by now. When I tell people that burritos as you know them here have zero resemblance to the burritos made in Sonora (and that very few Mexicans eat burritos outside of Chihuahua and Sonora because you wouldn't catch a Mexican eating rice and beans inside a tortilla), I feel like the Grim Reaper, crushing culinary dreams left, right and centre.

I have always felt that it is my duty to showcase Mexican food in Ireland as it should be, with as much respect for the origins of the dishes that I make as possible. At Picado, I teach traditional Mexican food. We share stories, culture and history around the table. People learn to cook Mexican food pretty much the same way every Mexican learns to cook it: by standing around the stove, watching someone experienced cooking and listening to the stories behind the dish, peppered with skilful instructions on how to make it.

For example, you can download a recipe for mole anywhere on the internet, but learning what mole means – how it evolved from its precolonial form, the role of colonial convent kitchens in mole's history, hearing the political context that surrounded the moles of the Baroque period in Mexico, the background of the women who created the recipes and the myths that surround the dish – is what makes cooking the mole recipe relevant. All that knowledge together with its context means it is no longer just a recipe. The stories enhance the flavour of the dish, and when we sit down to eat, that context makes you appreciate it.

A recipe is nothing without its context, so throughout these pages, you'll find the reason for each of these recipes and the story or background for its inclusion in the book – starting with my skipped goat tacos.

SKIPPED GOAT TACOS

SERVES 4–6

I come from the land of cabrito (kid goat). My hometown of Monterrey is renowned for its cabrito tradition – there are so many restaurants that serve this regional specialty. This recipe has been tucked away in my diary for almost 20 years. My mother calls it cabrito al natural, where the meat is the centre of the dish. I promise you, this traditional cooking method is the tastiest way you'll ever eat goat meat in a tortilla! You need to brine the meat a day in advance, and while that might sound like a lot of work, it's actually quite easy. Plus the results are so worth it: deliciously golden brown, crisp skin and succulent, juicy meat with a slight hint of cumin and bay leaf. Give it a try, you won't be disappointed.

1.5kg kid goat shoulder, on the bone

100g table salt

1 tsp cumin seeds

1 tsp freshly ground black pepper

12 large bay leaves, fresh or dried

40ml sunflower oil

FOR THE TACOS:

16 corn tortillas, warmed (see pages 12–13)

pico de gallo, without the cucumber (page 62)

de árbol salsa roja (page 50)

lime wedges

Start by putting your meat in a large casserole or pot (but first make sure the pot fits in your fridge, as you'll have to store it there). Cover the meat with plenty of fresh water, about 2.5–5cm above the meat. Add the salt, cumin seeds, black pepper and six of the bay leaves and stir to combine. Cover the pot and store in the fridge overnight (or for at least 4 hours).

Cabrito is traditionally cooked over charcoal, but I've adapted this recipe to be cooked in the oven with almost identical results. So the following day, or once you're getting ready to cook your meat, get your oven ready. Readjust the racks in your oven – put one at the lowest level and fill a deep roasting tin with water. Add the remaining six bay leaves to the water and place the tin on the bottom rack.

The next rack will be the one your meat will cook on, so place it directly over the roasting tin. During the cooking process, this bay-scented water will boil and evaporate, keeping the meat moist and fragrant.

After you've adjusted your cooking racks (there's nothing worse than trying to rearrange them while your oven is hot), preheat your oven to 180°C.

Now get a second roasting tin with a cooking rack fitted on it. If you don't have one, use the one that came with your oven – just make sure to line it with foil so that the juices and fat dripping from the meat will be collected there and won't burn your tray. It's important that the meat is cooked directly on the rack so that the juices and fat drip down and don't accumulate around the meat.

While the oven preheats, take the meat out of the brine and rinse it lightly. Put it on a plate and rub the sunflower oil all over the meat, then place it on the rack you prepared, skin side up. Roast in the preheated oven for 2½ hours.

While the meat cooks, prepare the pico de gallo (but make sure to omit the cucumber as it's not needed for this taco) and the de árbol salsa roja.

Heat up your tortillas and bring all the components to the table. When the meat is done, just shred it with two forks into large chunks. Make sure to break the crisp skin into manageable bits so that people can add it to the tacos.

To assemble your tacos, add some delicious meat to a warm corn tortilla, then a spoonful of pico de gallo, a drizzle of salsa and a little squeeze of lime juice – job done! And as you bite into it, spare a thought for all the 'skipped goats' of this world (see my story on pages 1–2) that don't have a chance to make tacos … because being a girl sucks sometimes.

BRINE OVERNIGHT

I recommend you brine the meat the day before you intend to cook it. Do it before going to bed and stick it in the fridge overnight for super succulent, tasty meat. Otherwise, give the meat at least 4 hours in the brine.

DRUNKEN BEEF BARBACOA TACOS

SERVES 4–6

Barbacoa tacos were my dad's favourite Sunday breakfast. He would get up at the crack of dawn to queue for the best barbacoa – if you arrive late, the best cuts are always sold out. He'd buy tons of the good salsa and some tortillas and by 10 a.m. the entire clan would gather around the table to eat. This recipe is an adaptation of my grandfather's, who was a butcher at one point in his life and who made a great barbacoa.

2kg rib steak (also known as chuck steak)

1 large onion, quartered

4 large garlic cloves, peeled and left whole

100ml white tequila

100ml water

2 tbsp dried Mexican oregano

1 tbsp table salt

3 large bay leaves, fresh or dried

FOR THE TACOS:

16 corn tortillas, warmed (see pages 12–13)

1 medium onion, finely diced

1 small bunch of fresh coriander, chopped (leaves and stems)

salsa verde (page 51)

Line the basket of your steamer with two large strips of foil in a criss-cross way (or see the tip on the next page to use a slow cooker instead). Make sure you have plenty of foil hanging over the sides of the steamer basket, as you'll be using the excess to fold up onto itself to create a parcel so that the beef steams in its own juices. Put the steak in the bottom of the lined basket and set aside.

Put the onion, garlic, tequila, water, oregano and salt in a blender or food processor and blitz for 30 seconds. It won't look smooth, as onions never blend completely, but it should all be well minced and combined. This is a powerful liquid, quite oniony and harsh, but don't worry, it's all good.

Pour the boozy, oniony liquid over the meat in the steamer basket, then add the bay leaves on top. Fold the overhanging foil strips towards the centre and twist the ends, creating a sort of loose but fully sealed parcel for the meat to cook in. Creating a well-sealed environment for the meat to gently stew and steam in is of paramount importance to a good barbacoa. If you rip the foil the juices will escape and the meat will dry out and burn, so be careful.

Pour hot water into the base of your steamer and place the basket on the pot. Cover with its lid and steam on a medium-low heat for 3½ hours, until the meat is completely tender and falling apart. I recommend checking the levels of hot water in the base of your steamer every

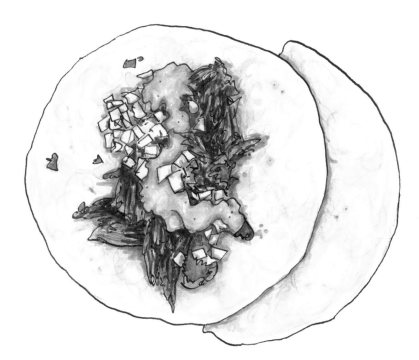

40 minutes or so to make sure it hasn't all evaporated or your pot will burn.

While the barbacoa cooks, get on with preparing the toppings and the salsa verde.

After the cooking time is up, carefully open the top of the foil parcel to check that the meat is ready – it should be fragrant and tender. Using tongs, transfer the meat to a heated bowl and spoon over some of the cooking juices. Shred it gently with a fork – it should fall apart easily – and keep warm.

Bring the warm tortillas and all the toppings to the table. To assemble your tacos, put some of the tender barbacoa into a warm corn tortilla, then top with some diced raw onion and chopped fresh coriander and drizzle with the salsa verde. Divine!

NO STEAMER? NO PROBLEM!

Most Mexicans steam barbacoa in the same pot they use to steam tamales, which is basically an oversized, deep basket steamer. However, a slow cooker will work perfectly too – just ditch the foil, put everything into the bowl of the slow cooker, add an extra 100ml of water to the recipe and cook it on a low setting overnight or on a high setting for 8 hours.

CARNE ASADA TACOS

SERVES 4–6

In my hometown of Monterrey, in the north-east of Mexico, families gather around the asador (the charcoal BBQ) every weekend to take part in a tradition that is almost sacred: making carne asada. In regio speak (regio is what people from Monterrey are referred to as), making carne asada is synonymous with having an informal party with family and friends, where meat and other delicious things will be grilled. It's always sunny in Monterrey, so the BBQ can be lit at any time. Irish weather is more unpredictable, so I use a skillet when it's miserable out and I want to remember what sunshine feels like. I use sirloin steak, but rib-eye steak or any meat suitable for grilling is good.

850g sirloin steak
(about 3 large steaks)

2 limes

¾ tsp garlic powder

¾ tsp freshly ground black pepper

flaky sea salt

½ small onion

vegetable oil, for brushing

FOR THE TACOS:

16 corn tortillas, warmed
(see pages 12–13)

1 small onion, finely diced

1 small bunch of fresh coriander, chopped (leaves and stems)

taquera salsa verde (page 52)

2 limes, quartered

Start by laying the steaks in a glass or non-reactive baking dish. Cut the limes in half and squeeze their juice over the steaks, then sprinkle over half the garlic powder, half the pepper and some salt to taste. Turn the steaks over and sprinkle the rest of the garlic powder, the remaining pepper and a little more salt on the other side. Let the meat marinate for at least 30 minutes but no more than 1 hour max, otherwise the lime will start cooking the meat. Leave it out at room temperature while it marinates to relax the muscle, giving you a more tender steak.

Heat up a cast iron skillet over a high heat for about 5 minutes. This is very important, as it will allow your steaks to sear properly, but try not to let the skillet get so hot that it smokes. It's not the end of the world if it does but it's a sure indication that the pan is very hot, so move on immediately to the next step.

Rub the skillet a few times with the cut side of the onion half. This will season your skillet with a lovely oniony flavour and will impart a nice aroma to your meat. I like to brush the onion on the last go with a little bit of vegetable oil and do the last rub with a slightly oily onion. The oil will also prevent your steaks from sticking to the skillet.

As soon as you finish with the onion, reduce the heat to medium-high, remove the steaks from the marinade and place them in your skillet. Do not overcrowd the skillet – depending on its size, you may have to cook just one or two steaks a time. I like my steak medium-rare and my steaks are about 5cm thick, so I cook them for 3 minutes on each side and it gives me perfect results. Cooking times depend on how thick your steak is and how done you like it to be, but roughly, for a rare steak cook it for 1½ minutes on each side, 3 minutes on each side for medium or 5 minutes per side for well done.

Remove the steak to a chopping board and cover loosely with foil. Let it rest for 5 minutes. This will allow the meat to relax again, release some of its juices and reabsorb them, giving you a tender, juicy steak. Reserve any cooking juices left on the board.

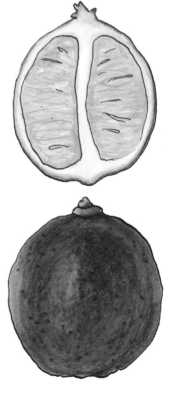

While the steak rests, warm up a serving plate so that you can place the meat on it after you cut it. Get all the trimmings for the tacos ready at the table and start heating your tortillas.

Slice the rested steak, always against the grain of the meat, and place the cut pieces on the warm plate. Pour any cooking juices from the board over the meat, then bring the plate to the table and call in the troops. Make a carne asada taco by putting a couple of slices of steak in a warmed corn tortilla, add some chopped onion and coriander and drizzle everything with a generous spoonful of salsa. Finish it off with a squeeze of lime juice.

TACOS AL PASTOR

SERVES 4–6

Tacos al pastor were born after an influx of Lebanese immigrants to Mexico City during the early 1900s. Traditionally cooked slowly on a shawarma, the result is deliciously juicy, bright red meat with a crisp edge and the right amount of spiciness and fruitiness – the pairing of chillies and citrus fruit is heavenly. This is my homemade version of the dish. It benefits from overnight marinating, but it works well if you give it at least 2 hours. Usually served in mini corn tortillas, topped with caramelised pineapple, raw onion, coriander and a good salsa, these tacos are a perfect example of how chillies are not all about heat, but mostly about flavour.

2kg pork tenderloin, cut into thin strips

60ml sunflower oil

FOR THE AL PASTOR SAUCE:

30g dried guajillo chillies

20g dried ancho chillies

1 large plum tomato

170g fresh pineapple, cut into chunks

3 chipotle chillies in adobo sauce

2 large garlic cloves, peeled

1 small onion, quartered

75ml apple cider vinegar

juice of 2 medium oranges

3 cloves

1 tsp cumin seeds

1 tsp dried Mexican oregano

1 tsp flaky sea salt

Start by making the al pastor sauce. Remove the stems from the dried chillies and cut them with scissors along the side to butterfly them. Remove all the seeds and veins and discard. Rehydrate by putting them in a saucepan with 1 litre of water and bringing to the boil, then lower the heat and simmer for 8–10 minutes, until very soft. Drain and allow to cool completely, then transfer to a blender or food processor.

Meanwhile, put a dry skillet or frying pan on a high heat and place the whole tomato on it, turning it every 2 minutes or so to make sure it chars all over and is fully roasted – this takes about 8 minutes.

Add the rest of the sauce ingredients, including the charred tomato, to the chillies in the blender or food processor and blitz until smooth. Taste to check the heat – if you want it hotter, just add more chipotles in adobo sauce and blend again.

Put the pork strips in a large bowl and pour over the sauce. Mix well, making sure you coat all the meat. Cover and refrigerate overnight or for at least 2 hours.

Heat a medium-sized non-stick frying pan over a high heat. Add half of the fresh pineapple cubes and cook for 3–4 minutes, stirring gently to cook them on all sides, until the

FOR THE TACOS:

250g fresh pineapple, cut into small bite-sized cubes

16 corn tortillas, warmed (see pages 12–13)

1 medium onion, finely diced

1 small bunch of fresh coriander (leaves only)

lime wedges

de árbol salsa roja (page 50)

juice has dried out. The cubes should be brown all over and smell very sweet. Transfer to a serving bowl and let it cool down while you cook the next batch in the same pan. Set the caramelised cubes aside to cool to room temperature for serving.

To cook the pork, heat a large non-stick frying pan over a high heat and add one-third of the sunflower oil. Depending on the size of your pan, you might need to do this in two or three batches, so you won't use the sunflower oil all at once.

When the oil and pan are piping hot, add one-third of the meat with its sauce to the pan. Cook on a high heat for 5–6 minutes, until the sauce starts to dry up. Stir occasionally to make sure the meat cooks and browns evenly. The entire process takes about 15 minutes. I always have a large ovenproof bowl in the oven at around 150°C and use that to keep the meat hot while I cook the next batch.

Repeat until all your meat is cooked, scraping the pan gently in between batches to save all the burnt bits – the fruit juice adds a delicious charred flavour to the meat, so throw them in with the cooked meat in the bowl. Once all the pork has been cooked, that bowl can be brought straight to the table.

Heat your tortillas while the last batch of meat is cooking. Mix the onion and coriander together in little serving bowls with spoons. Place a plate of lime wedges on the table along with the salsa and the caramelised pineapple cubes you made earlier.

To assemble your tacos, add some pork to a warm corn tortilla. Top with onion and coriander, caramelised pineapple, a generous drizzle of salsa and a good squeeze of lime juice. Enjoy with a cold beer and thank the gods for the Mexican genius who looked at a shawarma and thought, 'Feck the lamb, I need some pork with a spicy sauce to cook in that contraption!'

PORK PIBIL TACOS

SERVES 4–6

I always think of pork pibil as the dish that conquered Irish hearts: first the hearts of my Irish family, and later on the hearts of every person who came to Picado's tortilla class and fell in love with its simplicity and wonderful flavours. I normally make mine in a pressure cooker, which, together with a blender, is an essential item in every Mexican kitchen. However, I wanted to create a slow-roasted version of the dish, one cooked in the oven on a bed of banana leaves. I dare you not to fall in love with this recipe too.

2 fresh banana leaves (or parchment paper – see the note on page 27)

1kg pork shoulder, skin left on, cut into three chunks

350g ripe tomatoes, cut into quarters

1 small onion, peeled and cut into quarters

5 large garlic cloves, peeled and left whole

1 x 7cm Mexican cinnamon stick

½ tsp black peppercorns

50g Mexican achiote paste

75ml apple cider vinegar

juice of 1 large orange

1½ tsp flaky sea salt

80ml water

FOR THE TACOS:

16 corn tortillas, warmed (see pages 12–13)

de árbol salsa roja (page 50)

red onion pickle (page 60)

Preheat the oven to 150°C.

If you're not using the banana leaves, skip to the part of the recipe on page 26 where you place the pork in the casserole. If you are using the banana leaves, they must be cured to make them flexible and to get rid of their natural sap. This takes only a few minutes but it's essential, as if you use uncured banana leaves, the dish will take on the bitter taste of the sap.

Heat a large, dry frying pan over a high heat. Cut each banana leaf in half – they are usually around 1 metre long, so you'll end up with four 50cm-long pieces. Using scissors, remove the hard stalk along the length of the leaves, making sure not to break them as they're delicate when uncured.

When the pan is very hot, place one of the leaf halves, bumpy side down, on the hot pan. Start at one end and move it along the pan the way you'd move pasta sheets along when making them fresh in a machine. Using a spatula, press the leaf against the hot pan for a few seconds until you see it changing colour. The green colour will deepen and you will hear a sizzling sound (that's the sap burning and it smells awful!).

Move the leaf along the pan until all the bumpy side has been cured, then flip it over and do the same thing on the opposite (smooth) side, which takes less time. You will notice the leaves getting softer, more pliable and easier to handle once they've been cured. Set aside while you cure the remaining pieces.

Once you've cured all your banana leaves, give the frying pan a quick wash to make sure no burnt sap remains on it, then put it back on a medium heat. Use the cured banana leaves to line a heavy-based cast iron casserole with a tight-fitting lid (or a small roasting tin) in a criss-cross manner, making sure some of each leaf is hanging over the sides, as you're going to use the overhanging bits to wrap up the meat like a parcel.

If you're not using banana leaves, start here!

Place the pieces of pork in the casserole, skin facing up so it doesn't stick. Add the tomato and onion quarters, wedging them in between the pieces of meat and on the top. Set aside and return to the hot pan.

Place the whole garlic cloves in the hot pan, turning them every minute or so – the aim is to have lovely golden garlic with plenty of charred bits and a sweet smell. This will take about 6 minutes. Halfway through, add the cinnamon stick to the same pan and toast it for 2–3 minutes before adding the peppercorns and toasting for 1 minute more, until they are fragrant. The kitchen should smell beautiful by now.

Transfer everything from the pan to a blender followed by the achiote paste, apple cider vinegar, orange juice, salt and 40ml of the water. Blend until smooth, then pour the sauce over the meat in the casserole. Use the remaining 40ml of water to rinse any leftover sauce out of the blender and pour this into the casserole too.

Tightly fold the overhanging banana leaves over the meat (or cover with a piece of parchment paper cut to fit your casserole) and cover the casserole with its lid. Transfer to the oven and roast for 3½ hours.

Take the casserole out of the oven and uncover the meat. Everything should be soft so, using two forks, shred the meat and crush the tomatoes and onions,

making sure to mix everything together – there should be enough sauce to coat everything well. The banana leaves are not edible, but they provide a lovely oily texture and some flavour to the dish. I normally just carry the casserole to the table and let the meat rest and soak up all the flavours of the sauce while I get everything else together.

Set the table and bring over bowls of the de árbol salsa roja and red onion pickle to add a little heat. To assemble your tacos, add some pork to a warm corn tortilla, then spoon over some of the salsa and red onion pickle.

TRY THIS

Always use fresh banana leaves, never frozen – the frozen ones are too slimy for my liking. I buy fresh banana leaves in Asia Market in Dublin, but if you can't find them, put a piece of parchment paper on top of the meat before covering with a tight-fitting lid.

POTATO & CHORIZO TACOS

SERVES 4–6

This taco filling is a classic that features in almost every Mexican cook's repertoire. I normally use raw chorizo sausage as opposed to the dry-cured Spanish chorizo we usually get in Ireland, but if all you have is Spanish chorizo, use it. This taco is the perfect introduction to Mexican food for a nervous or picky Irish eater because there are potatoes in it and chorizo is pretty common these days. I use Rooster potatoes as they're nice and sturdy, but Maris Pipers are a good waxy potato and baby potatoes work well too.

2 tbsp sunflower oil

600g potatoes (see the intro), peeled and cut into 1.5cm cubes

flaky sea salt

300g fresh or dry-cured chorizo, cut into small pieces

150g halved and thinly sliced onion

1 small fresh red jalapeño chilli, finely chopped

1 large ripe tomato, cut into small cubes

75ml pale ale

FOR THE TACOS:

smoky refried beans (page 57), warmed

16 corn tortillas, warmed (see pages 12–13)

de árbol salsa roja (page 50)

250g feta cheese, crumbled

Preheat the oven to a low heat for warming later on. Place an ovenproof serving bowl in the oven to warm up too.

Heat the oil in a large non-stick frying pan on a medium-high heat, then add the potatoes and season with flaky sea salt. Don't crowd the potatoes, so make sure your pan is large enough to hold the potatoes in a single layer (or cook them in batches). Cook for about 4 minutes, stirring occasionally, until browned on all sides. Stir in the chorizo, reduce the heat to medium and cook for 4–5 minutes, until the chorizo has released all its ruby juices. Stir occasionally to prevent sticking, but not too frequently as you don't want mushy potatoes.

Add the onion and chilli and continue to cook until the onion has softened a little. Add the tomato and beer and cook for a further 3 minutes, until the tomatoes have softened and the beer has reduced by half and turned everything into a reddish sauce. At this point, the potatoes should be soft but still have a little bit of bite to them.

Transfer the contents of the pan to the warmed serving bowl and return to the oven to keep warm while you get the rest of the taco components ready.

To assemble your tacos, add a spoonful of spicy refried beans to a warm corn tortilla, followed by a good amount of potato and chorizo filling. Crown with a drizzle of salsa and some crumbled feta cheese.

HOT HOT HOT

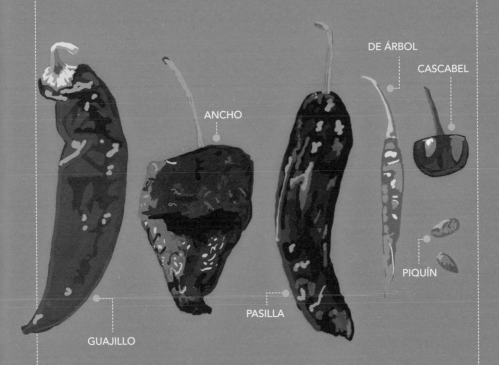

DE ÁRBOL

CASCABEL

ANCHO

PIQUÍN

PASILLA

GUAJILLO

Chillies vary so much in size, especially dried ones, that it's better to weigh them rather than say you should add a certain number of them to a recipe. For example, the de árbol chillies I have in my kitchen at the moment are tiny, so I'd need 20 chillies to make up the 10 grams called for in the de árbol and tamarind pork tacos on the next page, but a different batch might have bigger chillies, so if I put in 20 it would be too much (and way too hot!). This is why all my recipes list chillies in grams.

DE ÁRBOL & TAMARIND PORK TACOS

SERVES 4–6

This pork roast makes the most delicious tacos and the leftovers are a joy in a crusty bread roll with mayonnaise the following day. I usually make it early in the day or the day before, then I let it cool, chop it up and reheat it in a pan with some of its own juices to crisp up the skin and the meat. I cook the pork in a heavy-based cast iron casserole with a lid as it means less washing up, but you can do it in a roasting tin wrapped tightly with foil too.

2 tbsp sunflower oil

1.5kg pork shoulder, skin scored

flaky sea salt and freshly ground black pepper

FOR THE SAUCE:

1 tbsp sunflower oil

50g thickly sliced onion

15g pecan nuts

10g dried de árbol chillies, stemmed

1 large garlic clove, peeled

125ml Mexican tamarind syrup

50ml freshly squeezed orange juice

50ml pale ale

1½ tsp Worcestershire sauce

1½ tsp teriyaki sauce

1½ tsp flaky sea salt

Preheat the oven to 180°C.

Heat the oil in a heavy-based casserole on a medium-high heat. Season the pork well with salt and pepper, then add to the casserole and sear it on all sides until it turns a lovely brown colour. When you finish, make sure the meat is skin side up or else it will stick to the pot while it roasts. Reduce the heat to its lowest setting to keep the pot warm and get on with making the sauce.

To make the sauce, heat the oil in a small non-stick frying pan on a medium heat. Add the onion, pecans, chillies and garlic and cook gently for 4–5 minutes, stirring regularly to avoid burning the chillies. The onion should be soft, the garlic and the pecans golden and the chillies a gorgeous shade of auburn.

Transfer the contents of the pan, including every drop of oil, to a blender or food processor. Add the rest of the sauce ingredients and blend until completely smooth.

Pour the sauce over the meat, making sure some of it goes under the meat and over the sides. Cover the casserole with a tight-fitting lid (or wrap a roasting tin tightly in foil) and transfer to the preheated oven. Roast for 70 minutes, then remove the lid or foil, baste the meat and cook, uncovered, for a further 20 minutes to caramelise the sauce. Remove from the oven and set aside until the pork is cool enough to handle.

FOR THE TACOS:

16 corn tortillas, warmed (see pages 12–13)

Mexican slaw (page 59)

Don Paulino Mexican hot sauce or your favourite hot sauce

Take the meat out of the sauce and cut thick slices of the roast, then cut again into bite-sized cubes. Don't forget to include the layer of skin here, as it will add a ton of flavour and crunch to your tacos. Transfer the cubes to a large bowl. Scrape every bit of the sauce from the casserole into the bowl and mix well to cover every morsel of meat with the sticky sauce. Now it's time to decide how much of the deliciously sticky meat you will use for your tacos and how much you want for leftovers (I love planning my leftovers in advance!). Once you know, get on with the last step.

Heat a large non-stick frying pan over a high heat. The cooking sauce will already have plenty of fat from the meat, so you don't need to use any extra oil. When the pan is very hot, add the cubed pork (working in batches if necessary so you don't overcrowd the pan) and cook, stirring regularly, for 8–10 minutes. The meat should be crisp, moist and sticky from the caramelised sauce. Transfer to a warmed serving bowl.

Set the table and bring over the bowl of Mexican slaw and the hot sauce. The last step between you and these delicious tacos is assembly, which is dead easy: grab a warm corn tortilla, add some sticky meat, top it with some slaw and add a few drops of hot sauce.

CHICKEN CHICHARRÓN TACOS

SERVES 4–6

This is not a traditional Mexican taco by any stretch of the imagination. It was born out of my pure and unadulterated love for all things crispy and inspired by the flavours of Asia, but with every element that makes a taco great: acidity, crunch and heat. I normally use tequila reposado or añejo for the recipe, as that's all I ever have in my pantry, but tequila blanco is perfectly adequate too. Always use chicken with skin on, as it will give you a crunchier exterior and will keep the chicken moist as it cooks. I serve this with my sticky hibiscus and chipotle salsa – don't skip it, it's what makes these tacos awesome.

8 boneless chicken thighs (skin on)

4 tbsp tequila (I like reposado, but any tequila will do)

4 tsp grated fresh ginger

½ tsp chipotle powder

½ tsp table salt

1 tsp freshly ground black pepper

sunflower oil, for deep-frying

FOR THE SPICY COATING:

250g cornflour (cornstarch)

½ tsp chipotle powder

¼ tsp freshly ground black pepper

a pinch of flaky sea salt

Start by marinating the chicken. I usually do this the day before so that the chicken has time to really absorb these amazing flavours. Place the chicken thighs in a freezer bag with the tequila, ginger, chipotle powder, salt and pepper, then seal the bag, getting as much air out of it as possible. Massage the contents of the bag so that all the ingredients are well mixed, rubbing and coating each piece of chicken in the bag until the thighs are slightly reddish. Put the bag on a baking tray (in case of any spills) and place it in the fridge overnight. If you don't have the foresight (or patience, as I don't sometimes) for overnight marinating, give it at least 3 hours.

This is a good time to make the salsa on page 54 and to make the spicy coating by combining all the ingredients for it in a large bowl. Set aside.

When you're ready to fry the chicken, take it out of the fridge to allow it to come to room temperature, still in its bag.

You will also need to put a wire rack or cooling rack over a baking tray lined with kitchen paper. This is to rest your chicken once it's fried so that any excess oil drips on the kitchen paper and not on your counter.

Heat the oil in a deep-fryer to 190°C. I have a mini fryer that I adore that holds only 1.2 litres of oil, but if you don't have one, don't worry – this is totally doable in a medium-sized,

FOR THE TACOS:

sticky hibiscus and chipotle salsa (page 54), warmed

30g ready-salted peanuts, chopped

20g sesame seeds

16 corn tortillas, warmed (see pages 12–13)

Mexican slaw (page 59)

heavy-based pot or cast iron casserole; see the next page. (I always deep-fry in high-sided pots, not frying pans, as the walls of the pot take most of the splashes and it makes frying a little safer.)

While the oil is heating up, take one of the pieces of chicken and drop it into the bowl with the spicy coating, tossing to coat generously. Set aside and repeat until you have as many pieces of chicken coated as you are going to fry in one go (I do two at a time in my mini deep-fryer or four in my cast iron pot).

Using tongs, carefully lower the coated chicken into the hot oil. Cook for 15 minutes, turning the chicken a couple times during the cooking process. Use a timer, as no one wants raw or overcooked chicken. When the timer goes, remove the chicken carefully from the oil and place it on the prepared cooling rack. The chicken skin needs at least 5 minutes to finish crisping up, so resting the chicken like this will give you maximum crunch!

Repeat until all your chicken is fried. Don't worry, the chicken won't go cold. It stays quite hot on the cooling rack for the time it takes to fry it all.

Slice each chicken thigh into four or six small pieces (depending on how big the thighs are). Place the pieces on a wooden board or a heated serving plate and drizzle with some of the warmed sticky hibiscus and chipotle salsa. Sprinkle some of the chopped peanuts and sesame seeds over the chicken, then bring it to the table with the rest of the components for your tacos. I usually combine the rest of the chopped peanuts and sesame seeds in one bowl with a spoon and leave it at the table.

To assemble your tacos, place a couple of chicken pieces in a warm corn tortilla. Drizzle with more salsa, add some more peanuts and sesame seeds and top with a small portion of Mexican slaw. This taco is heaven on a plate!

HOW TO

TEST THE TEMPERATURE OF OIL IF YOU DON'T HAVE A DEEP-FRYER

Put the pot or casserole on the hob and add the sunflower oil. The amount of oil depends on how big your pot is and how many pieces of chicken you're frying at a time. I use a cast iron pot that can cook four thighs at a time, so I use about 2 litres of oil. I start the heat at medium, then after a couple of minutes I crank it up to medium-high, then a minute later to high. The secret to getting perfect chicken chicharrón is having the oil at a constant 190°C. This is easy to do with a deep-fryer, but if you're using a high-sided pot, you can do a few things:

1 USE A CANDY THERMOMETER

Submerge the thermometer in the oil, clip it to the edge of the pot and allow the oil to reach the desired temperature (try not to rest it touching the bottom of the pot, as the temperature of the pot itself will always be higher and it won't give you an accurate reading of the oil). These thermometers are very affordable and handy to have in your kitchen.

2 THE WOODEN SPOON METHOD

Submerge the tip of the handle of a wooden spoon into the oil. If bubbles start forming around it, the oil is ready (bubbles form because the natural moisture and air in the wood are released when hot oil is introduced). This method worked okay for me before I got a thermometer.

3 THE ONION SLICE METHOD

My mother does this all the time (she laughs at my thermometer!). When you see ripples in the oil, drop in a single small slice of onion. If it bubbles and immediately rises to the top of the oil, the temperature is perfect. (Regardless of what my mother says, this is not scientifically accurate!)

CHICKEN TACOS DORADOS

SERVES 4–6

This taco brings back childhood memories with every bite. My mother used to make them at least once a week for us as children because they were our favourite meal. In the winter she served them with a side of chicken soup, made with the stock she cooked the chicken in. It's still my go-to meal when I feel homesick.

4 large chicken breasts

¼ small onion, cut into two chunks

2 large garlic cloves, peeled

2 bay leaves, dried or fresh

1 tsp table salt

2 litres water

FOR THE TACOS:

16 corn tortillas, warmed (see pages 12–13)

sunflower oil, for deep-frying

Mexican slaw (page 59)

2 ripe tomatoes, halved and sliced

¼ onion, thinly sliced

de árbol salsa roja (page 50)

250ml crème fraîche, thinned with a splash of milk

Put the chicken, onion, garlic, bay leaves, salt and water in a large pot and bring to the boil. Lower the heat and simmer for 40 minutes, until the chicken is fully cooked and tender. Remove it from the liquid and shred it using two forks. Set aside to fill your tacos.

While the chicken cooks, get on with prepping the Mexican slaw and other toppings so that you have those ready to serve.

Preheat your oven to 100°C and put a baking tray in the oven to heat up too. Line a large plate with some kitchen paper to rest your tacos on after they're fried.

Take a warm corn tortilla and fill it with a handful of cooked shredded chicken, spreading it horizontally along the bottom half of the tortilla (the half that's closest to you). This will make folding the taco easier. Do not overfill your tacos at this point – leave room for all the other bits that will go into the taco later on.

Using your hands, fold the tortilla in half to encase the filling and to give it the classic taco shape. Secure the fold with a toothpick to stitch the top of your taco together. Set the taco aside on a plate and cover it with a clean tea towel while you continue filling and folding the rest of the tortillas.

DON'T DEEP-FRY

I don't like using a deep-fryer for frying these tacos as too much oil is wasted for my liking. Plus, not having a bottom for the taco to sit on (like it does on a frying pan) can result in the taco getting puffy and the filling slipping out of it. If you want to cook the tacos in bigger batches, just use a bigger frying pan.

Heat the sunflower oil in a small frying pan over a high heat. In order to crisp up the tacos quickly and avoid any sogginess, make sure the oil is very hot before you start frying in it – I keep mine at around 180°C. Gently lower a couple of tacos into the hot oil and fry for 1½–2 minutes on each side. The tacos should be golden brown and crisp.

Using kitchen tongs to prevent any splashes of hot oil, lift out the tacos and allow any excess oil to drip back into the pan. Set them on the plate lined with kitchen paper for a few seconds to absorb any excess oil, then remove the toothpick in the taco and immediately transfer them to the baking tray in the oven so they remain warm. Repeat with the rest of the tacos until they are all fried.

To serve, bring everything to the table and let people fill their own tacos. Grab a taco, carefully open it from the top and add some Mexican slaw, slices of tomato and onion, salsa and crème fraîche. Eat them with your hands – it's messy, but so worth it!

THE BATTLE OF THE CRUNCH

TACO SHELLS
VS.
FRIED TACOS

There is a BIG difference between a taco dorado and a taco shell. First of all, taco shells are not Mexican – they're a Tex-Mex invention and they belong to the crappy 'world cuisine' aisle of a run-of-the-mill supermarket along with all the other poor, cheap imitations of international cuisines coming out of factories with zero knowledge of the food but loads of clever marketing executives.

Taco shells have been designed to be shelf stable. The shell is partly cooked and needs to be finished off before it becomes a crisp shell. But when you bake these things, oil comes out of them. No amount of soaking a real corn tortilla in oil will ever do that naturally or render that same result. If you leave a corn tortilla sitting in a puddle of oil, it will fall apart and disintegrate. They will never behave that way naturally. That's the end of my rant.

Tacos dorados, on the other hand, are a wonderful Mexican dish that features in households, markets and small restaurants all over the country. They are fully formed tacos, i.e. a warmed corn tortilla filled with something tasty, that is then shallow-fried until crisp. When it comes to flavour, there is no comparison whatsoever between the industrial shells and tacos dorados. Homemade all the way! You know what oil you're using and how much of it. They're also sturdier on account of a proper corn tortilla being used, so they will fill you up more than the processed ones. There is less salt, less fat and way more flavour.

So if you're a fan of the shop-bought shells, prepare to be amazed – these chicken tacos dorados are the real thing. You can thank me later.

ENSENADA-STYLE FISH TACOS

SERVES 4–6

These tacos are summer on a plate. Super tasty, playful and colourful, you'll want to have them again and again. Using the freshest fish renders the best results. In Mexico we use angel shark, dogfish or tilapia fish, but in Ireland I go for monkfish or cod. The taco has quite a few toppings, so I suggest you make all of them first, then start the batter. While the batter rests in the fridge, you can prep the fish. When you finally cook it, everything will be ready with no delay between the fish coming out of the pan and going to the table.

FOR THE BATTER:

350g plain flour

2 tbsp baking powder

1 tsp dried Mexican oregano

½ tsp garlic granules

½ tsp onion salt

½ tsp flaky sea salt

½ tsp freshly ground black pepper

1 egg, cold from the fridge

450ml pale ale, lager or sparkling water, very cold (you might need a little more)

Prepare the batter by putting the flour, baking powder, spices, salt and pepper in a large bowl and whisking well. Crack the egg into the centre and gradually pour in the beer while you whisk vigorously for about 40 seconds. Make sure both the egg and the beer or sparkling water are very cold, as this will give you a better batter. Depending on the day you might need a little more beer or water to loosen up the batter, but start with the 450ml and decide if you need more once everything is incorporated. What you're looking for is a thickish batter that resembles the one used to make American pancakes. Rest the batter in the fridge for 15 minutes.

While the batter rests, get on with prepping your fish. Cut the tails lengthwise into strips about 2.5cm thick and 8–10cm long (you can always ask your fishmonger to do this for you). This will give you a fish goujon that you can comfortably cradle in a small corn tortilla. There's nothing more annoying than a fish goujon that's too big for your tortilla, as it makes eating the taco with all its toppings way too messy.

Place the fish strips on a baking tray and pat dry with kitchen paper (removing any moisture will allow the batter to stick better). Season with the salt and pepper on all sides and set aside.

FOR THE FISH:

1kg monkfish tails

1 tsp flaky sea salt

1 tsp freshly ground black pepper

sunflower oil, for deep-frying

FOR THE TACOS:

16 corn tortillas, warmed (see pages 12–13)

Mexican slaw (page 59)

pico de gallo (page 62)

red onion pickle (page 60)

chipotle mayonnaise (page 65)

Heat the oil in your deep-fryer or a wide, shallow, heavy-based casserole to 175°C (see page 34 for more options on how to check oil temperature without a thermometer).

While the oil heats, set a wire cooling rack on a baking tray lined with kitchen paper. This is where you'll rest the fish goujons after frying to allow the excess oil to drip off and keep the fish crisp.

Once the oil is almost at temperature, take the batter from the fridge and give it a good 20-second whisk.

Take a fish strip and dip it into the batter. Use tongs to swirl the fish in the batter so it gathers plenty of it, then gently drop it into the hot oil to fry. Repeat this step until you have reached the capacity of your deep-fryer or casserole, but don't crowd the fish, as it will puff a little – leave enough room to be able to turn them comfortably with a slotted spoon or another set of tongs. Fry for 5–6 minutes, turning the strips a couple of times during the cooking process. You should have golden brown, crisp goujons.

Transfer to the wire rack and keep making goujons until you've done them all. On your second to last batch, start heating up the tortillas and getting all the toppings to the table. Once the last batch is ready, transfer the fish to a serving plate and bring it straight to the table too.

To assemble your tacos, put some slaw in the centre of a warm corn tortilla. Top with a fish goujon, some pico de gallo, some red onion pickle and a good drizzle of chipotle mayonnaise. These tacos are finger-licking good, but be polite and have plenty of napkins available.

SWEET POTATO & CARROT TINGA

SERVES 4–6

So there I was with a full cooking class sitting at Picado's long table about five years ago, getting ready to make chicken tinga, when someone said, 'I'm a vegan, I can't eat that.' Normally we would know about any dietary restrictions in advance, but this time, the person forgot to tell us. I went into a panic, turned around and found sweet potatoes and carrots in the veggie bowl. With all the confidence in the world, I said, 'Not a problem, I've got you covered!' This recipe was the result, and I must say that it was such a success that I've continued to tweak it over the years and it has remained one of our favourite veggie/vegan tacos to date.

500g tomato passata (without any added flavours)

3 chipotle chillies in adobo sauce (or more if you want it spicier)

3 tbsp sunflower oil

100g halved and thinly sliced onion

2 large garlic cloves, finely chopped

4 sprigs of fresh thyme, leaves only

200g sweet potato, peeled and julienned

100g carrots, julienned

flaky sea salt and freshly ground black pepper

FOR THE TACOS:

16 corn tortillas, warmed (see pages 12–13)

shredded iceberg lettuce

crème fraîche (or a good-quality vegan natural yogurt or sour cream)

Put the passata and chipotles in a blender or food processor and blend until smooth, then taste to decide if you want it spicier or not. Remember that chipotles in adobo sauce develop a deeper heat when you cook them, so don't make it to the limit of your spice level at this point as it's going to get hotter as it cooks. Also, this tinga develops more heat a day or so after cooking it, so if you make it in advance, don't make it too spicy!

Heat the oil in a large non-stick frying pan over a medium-high heat. Add the onion, garlic and thyme and cook, stirring frequently, for a couple minutes, until the onions are translucent.

Add the sweet potatoes and carrots and cook for 3–4 minutes to brown them a little. Pour the chipotle tomato sauce over the veggies, stirring to incorporate everything together. Season with salt and pepper to taste. Lower the heat to medium and cook for 5 minutes, stirring occasionally, until the vegetables have softened a little but still have a little bit of bite to them.

While the tinga cooks, start heating your tortillas and bring everything to the table.

To assemble your tacos, add a spoonful of the tinga and a little shredded lettuce to a warm corn tortilla, then drizzle everything with a cooling amount of crème fraîche.

ROASTED BUTTERNUT SQUASH WITH ANCHO CHILLI CRUST TACOS
SERVES 4–6

I love this taco because it ticks every single box in the deliciousness department: it has heat, sweetness, depth of flavour, caramelisation and texture. When we had the famous crew of the American TV programme *F*ck, That's Delicious* at Picado for the filming of the Dublin episode, one of the guys described this taco as 'vegetarian bone marrow' and it made so much sense to me – it has that same richness and creaminess.

FOR THE ANCHO CHILLI CRUST:

1 litre water

45g dried ancho chillies

100ml sunflower oil

3 large garlic cloves, peeled

½ tsp anise seeds

½ tsp flaky sea salt

FOR THE ROASTED SQUASH:

2 butternut squash

2 tbsp roughly chopped ready-salted peanuts

2 tbsp sesame seeds

FOR THE TACOS:

16 corn tortillas, warmed (see pages 12–13)

Mexican slaw (page 59)

salsa madura (page 56)

citrusy crema (page 64)

Preheat the oven to 225°C. (I use a fan oven, which in my opinion provides crispier results, but a regular conventional oven works fine too.)

Put the water in a medium-sized pot and bring to the boil.

Heat a dry frying pan over a medium-high heat. While this happens, remove the stems of the ancho chillies and using scissors, butterfly them by cutting along the side of the chilli to open it up. Remove all the seeds and bits of veins from the chilli and discard them. Toast the chillies lightly in the hot pan for literally 3 seconds on each side – this will release the essential oils in the chillies, making them more fragrant and soft. Do not leave them on the hot pan for more than a few seconds or they will burn and acquire a bitter taste that will spoil the recipe.

As you take them out of the pan, place them into the pot of now-boiling water. Boil the chillies for 8 minutes. This will rehydrate the chillies, remove any natural bitterness and give you a smoother paste.

As soon as the chillies are done, discard the cooking water and transfer the chillies into a blender or food processor. (This water is awfully bitter, so don't be thinking it would make a nice chilli consommé!) Add the oil, garlic, anise seeds and salt and blend until you have a silky-smooth paste. You may need to scrape down the sides of your

blender a couple of times to make sure everything blends well. It's important to do this while the chillies are still piping hot, as it helps to emulsify the paste. Transfer the paste to a bowl and set aside.

Wash the unpeeled squashes well and dry them. Cut each squash in half lengthways, then into halves again – you should end up with four large wedges per squash. Score the flesh gently with a sharp knife as if you were scoring meat, making sure not to go all the way down into the skin.

Place each wedge of squash, scored side up and skin side down, on a baking tray, making sure they are snug but preferably not touching each other.

Using a pastry brush or the back of a spoon, paint the exposed sides of the squash with a thick layer of the ancho chilli paste. This layer will dry out and become crusty, flavouring your squash deliciously and giving it a great texture.

Roast the squash in the preheated oven for 40–45 minutes. The squash should be tender and the ancho chilli paste must be dark and almost crusty. Remove from the oven, transfer to a warm serving plate and sprinkle the chopped peanuts and sesame seeds on top.

While the squash cooks, get on with all the toppings so that they're ready by the time the squash comes out of the oven. With about 15 minutes left to go, start heating the tortillas. Bring all the toppings to the table.

To assemble your tacos, add some Mexican slaw to a warm corn tortilla, then scoop some of the tender squash on top and drizzle a tiny bit of the hot salsa over it. If you're worried about the heat use only a few drops of salsa, but don't omit it, it makes a huge difference as the squash would be way too sweet otherwise. Finally, cool everything down with some citrusy crema. You'll be in veggie taco heaven!

THREE WAYS WITH
TAJÍN

Tajín is the name of a seasoning company founded in 1985 in Jalisco, Mexico. Their first seasoning, a chilli and lime powder, has become synonymous with the brand, a bit like hoovers and vacuum cleaners. The seasoning is made with a mixture of dried chillies, lime and salt. You can make a homemade version and alternative brands like Valentina make a similar product, but true believers say that nothing compares. I used to mix powdered guajillo and piquín chillies with salt and lime powder before I had the shop, but to be honest, it's just as easy to buy Tajín. Here are three ways to use it.

1 FRUITY

Sprinkle Tajín generously over slices of tropical fruit like pineapple and mango as well as watermelon, oranges, melon, apples and cucumber.

2 BOOZY

Tajín on the rim of a margarita glass (instead of the salt) is to die for! It's also absolutely essential on the rim of a beer glass for micheladas.

3 CRUNCHY

My favourite way to use Tajín is to sprinkle it over hot popcorn. Trust me, you'll never look back.

SPICY BEAN & PAN-ROASTED CORN TACOS

SERVES 4–6

This taco was inspired by the traditional side dish of beans with corn, normally served as an accompaniment to carne en su jugo, a traditional meat stew from the city of Guadalajara, Mexico. I coupled plenty of creative licence here with my love for the two main components of that dish: beans and corn. This taco is both joyous and delicious and hopefully honours the flavours of the original side dish.

A note on corn: in Mexico we eat savoury corn, not the sweet varieties you find in Ireland. Savoury corn does not have the same flavour or texture as sweetcorn. We stock Mexican tinned corn at Picado and it works really well for this recipe, but when Irish sweetcorn is in season, I make a point of using it because it's so good! If you are completely stuck, frozen corn would work too, although the cooking time is a bit longer and the texture is chewier.

4 fresh red jalapeños or Kenyan chillies

4 tbsp sunflower oil

800g tinned Mexican corn, drained (or 800g frozen corn or 4 large fresh ears of corn, kernels cut off)

flaky sea salt

FOR THE TACOS:

2 batches of smoky refried beans (page 57)

16 corn tortillas, warmed (see pages 12–13)

250g feta cheese, crumbled

Tajín chilli and lime powder (optional)

You're going to need to make a double batch of the smoky refried beans on page 57 first and then get on with the rest of this recipe, but it's totally worth it.

Take the stems out of the chillies, then cut them in half lengthwise. Remove the placenta of the chillies and the seeds (I would rarely do this myself, but it does work better for what we need these chillies for). The placenta is the technical name for the lump of white membrane found close to the stem of the chillies as well as the veins that grow upwards out of it. Once the chillies are just flesh, i.e. no seeds or placenta left, cut them lengthwise into thin strips.

Heat the oil in a medium-sized non-stick frying pan over as high a heat as your hob can go. Add the chilli strips and cook until they have darkened in colour and developed a few blisters on their skin.

When the chilli strips are done, take them out with tongs and shake any excess oil back into the pan (which, by the way, is still on a high heat and will remain so). Take half of the now slightly red and chilli-infused oil out of the pan and reserve it for later.

Return the pan with the remaining oil back to the high heat and add half the corn kernels. Let them cook undisturbed until they start jumping a little (after all, they are descendants of popcorn varieties). Using a spatula or a spoon, stir the corn to cook it on all sides. The aim here is to char the corn kernels quite a bit. Depending on which type of corn you're using, it could take anywhere between 6 and 12 minutes. Frozen corn will release all its water first, so it will take longer to start caramelising. Fresh corn cooks a lot quicker and tinned Mexican corn is somewhere in the middle. The oil you left in the pan will infuse the corn with chilli flavours and help with the caramelisation. Season the corn with flaky sea salt halfway through cooking.

When the corn is golden and charred, transfer it to a warmed serving bowl. Return the pan to the high heat, add the chilli oil you reserved from earlier and the rest of the corn and repeat the process above until all the corn is cooked.

Start heating the tortillas and the spicy refried beans. Bring them to the table with the feta cheese and the strips of chilli you made at the beginning.

To assemble your tacos, add a spoonful of warm refried beans to a warm corn tortilla. Top those with a generous amount of corn, some feta, a strip or two of the fried chilli and a sprinkle of Tajín chilli and lime powder (if you're using it). Delicious!

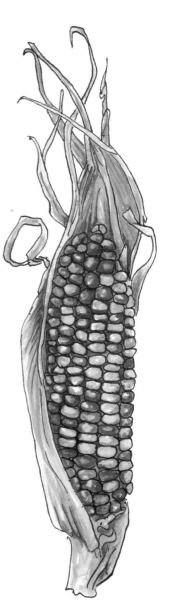

TOO HOT TO HANDLE

In Mexico the technique of frying chillies to blister them is called torear, but we do it with whole chillies. I was tempted to use whole chillies here but I reckoned that would be too much for the Irish palate, so strips, although more finicky, work better.

MUSHROOM CHILORIO TACOS

SERVES 4–6

Chilorio is a hugely popular dish from the Sinaloa region in Mexico. It's traditionally made with pork, but in recent years, as we move towards a more meat-free diet, you will find loads of recipes made with meat alternatives. I prefer to keep it all natural, so I love this version with mushrooms. I use a mix of mushrooms for both texture and flavour.

FOR THE SAUCE:

40g dried pasilla chillies

150ml water

50ml white wine vinegar

2 large garlic cloves, peeled

6 black peppercorns

2 tsp dried Mexican oregano

1 tsp coriander seeds

¼ tsp cumin seeds

½ tsp flaky sea salt

FOR THE MUSHROOM FILLING:

500g mixed fresh mushrooms (see the tip on the next page)

2 tbsp olive oil

150g halved and thinly sliced onion

FOR THE TACOS:

16 corn tortillas, warmed (see pages 12–13)

raw onion slices

1 small bunch of fresh coriander, leaves only

lime wedges

Fill a medium-sized pot with water and bring to the boil.

Start by cleaning the dried chillies. Remove the stems, then using a pair of scissors, cut along the side of the chillies to butterfly them. Remove all the seeds and veins. Drop the cleaned chillies into the boiling water and boil at a high heat for 5–8 minutes to rehydrate the chillies and sterilise them at the same time.

While the chillies cook, take a sharp knife and thinly slice all your mushrooms. However, if you're using oyster mushrooms (which I totally recommend you do), don't slice them, but instead tear them into thin strips. They'll look like shredded meat when they're cooked and it's a better way to treat them, as slicing them won't work as well. Set aside.

Drain the chillies and transfer them into a blender or food processor with the rest of the ingredients for the sauce. Blend everything until you have a smooth sauce. Set aside.

Heat the oil in a large non-stick frying pan over a medium heat for 1 minute. Add the onion slices and cook for 1 minute before adding the mushrooms. Cook gently for 2 minutes, then add the sauce. Continue to cook for a further 8–10 minutes, until the sauce is silky-smooth and shiny and every mushroom has been coated. Season with salt to taste.

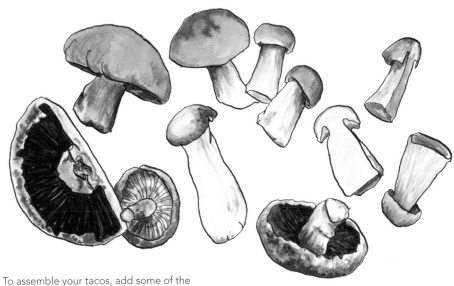

To assemble your tacos, add some of the mushroom filling to a warm corn tortilla, then top with slices of raw onion, coriander leaves and a squeeze of lime juice. I don't eat avocados anymore (see page 53 for more on that), but if you must, a thin slice of avocado will be tasty on this taco too.

MIX IT UP

I use a mixture of mushrooms that varies with the season and with what's available: porcini, shiitake, cremini, white button, oyster – just about anything that's fresh and looks good. However, I stay away from portobello mushrooms, as they tend to fall apart a little in this dish.

DE ÁRBOL SALSA ROJA

SERVES 4–6

This is the salsa we make at home when we want something tasty that goes with loads of things. It's great on eggs, steamed potatoes or with tortilla chips. You can make it as hot or as mild as you want by adjusting the amount of chilli in it – using 5 grams of dried de árbol chillies makes a medium-hot salsa (well, it's medium-hot to me anyway!). The secret is to cook it in a small pan with a tight-fitting lid; trust me on that.

2 tsp olive oil

450g medium-sized ripe vine tomatoes

5g dried de árbol chillies

2 spring onions, ends trimmed

1 large garlic clove, peeled and left whole

1 vegetable stock cube

1 small bunch of fresh coriander

flaky sea salt, to taste

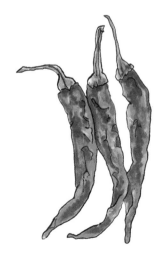

Heat the oil in a small non-stick frying pan (one with a tight-fitting lid) over a high heat. Add the tomatoes, chillies, spring onions and garlic. You might need to cut the spring onions in half so that they fit in the pan, but everything else goes in whole. As soon as it starts to sizzle, cover the pan with its lid and lower the heat to medium.

Set a timer for 20 minutes and resist the temptation to lift the lid during this time. This is super important, as the condensation that builds up inside the pan goes into the lid and then drops back into the tomatoes, showering them with moisture and giving your salsa the right consistency.

Once the timer goes, your tomatoes should have burst a little and be fully cooked. Transfer the contents of the pan, including every bit of juice and oil, into a blender or food processor. Add the stock cube and the coriander (stems and all) and blend everything together until you have a smooth, creamy salsa. Check for seasoning and adjust as necessary. I never add salt to this salsa until I taste it first, as some stock cubes can be quite salty.

This salsa lasts for a week in the fridge, covered. I don't particularly like freezing tomato-based salsas, as the texture is never right afterwards, so if you have leftovers, think of creative ways to use it in your meals. It's so good, you won't have a problem!

SALSA VERDE

SERVES 4–6

This is a family recipe that I go back to again and again as it's so delicious and simple. Tomatillos are naturally tangy and acidic with a flavour that complements loads of different dishes. It cuts through fatty meat-based fillings, but it also enhances subtle, delicate ones. I particularly love it with the barbacoa tacos on page 18.

2 tsp olive oil

800g tinned tomatillos, drained

2 fresh green jalapeño chillies

2 spring onions, ends trimmed

1 large garlic clove, peeled

1 small bunch of fresh coriander (optional)

flaky sea salt

Heat the oil in a small non-stick frying pan with a tight-fitting lid over a high heat. Add the tomatillos, chillies, spring onions and garlic. You might need to cut the spring onions in half so they fit in the pan, but everything else goes in whole. As soon as it starts to sizzle, cover the pan with its lid and lower the heat to medium.

Set a timer for 20 minutes and resist the temptation to lift the lid during this time. This is super important, as the condensation that builds up inside the pan goes into the lid and then drops back into the tomatillos, showering them with moisture and giving your salsa the right consistency.

Once the timer goes, everything should look a slightly paler shade of green and there should be plenty of liquid in the pan. Transfer the contents of the pan, including every bit of juice and oil, into a blender or food processor. Add the coriander (if using), stems and all, and a pinch of flaky sea salt and blend until you have a smooth, creamy salsa. Taste for seasoning and adjust as necessary.

This salsa lasts for a week in the fridge, covered. I normally use it over fried eggs the following day if I have any left. I don't particularly like freezing salsas, but this one actually freezes quite well, probably on account of the high acidity of the tomatillos.

TAQUERA SALSA VERDE

SERVES 4–6

This salsa is a favourite of many taco stands in my hometown of Monterrey. It's lusciously creamy, tangy and has a good level of heat, perfect for any grilled meats, especially the carne asada tacos on page 20.

Ever since avocados became the darling of superfoods all over the world they have become prohibitively expensive for many Mexicans, so people have found creative ways to add creaminess in salsas without avocados. This is a great example of that inventiveness: the clever addition of courgettes, which are plentiful and cheap in Mexico, results in a delicious, creamy salsa that does not sacrifice any flavour.

300g courgettes, thickly sliced

800g tinned tomatillos, drained

100ml water

2 tbsp sunflower oil

2 fresh green jalapeño chillies, cut into thick slices (with seeds)

1 large garlic clove, peeled

1 small bunch of fresh coriander (optional)

flaky sea salt

Place the courgettes, tomatillos and water in a medium-sized saucepan. I always put the courgettes at the bottom of the pot first to cook them better. Bring to the boil, then lower the heat to medium-high and cover the pan with a tight-fitting lid. Simmer for 20–25 minutes, until the courgettes are fully cooked.

Meanwhile, heat the oil in a small frying pan over a medium-high heat. Add the chilli slices and the whole garlic clove, then lower the heat to medium. Cook, stirring occasionally, for 8 minutes, until the chillies have blistered and changed to a lighter shade of green and the garlic is golden. The oil will become a light shade of green as it infuses with the lovely flavours of the chillies and garlic.

Transfer the contents of both the saucepan and the frying pan to a blender or food processor, making sure you scrape in every bit of oil from the pan as there is a lot of flavour in it. Follow with the coriander (if using), stems and all, and salt to taste. Blend until you have a completely smooth, creamy salsa.

I love the leftovers of this salsa on everything, but drizzled over baked potatoes is my absolute favourite way to use it. Keep it in the fridge in a sealed jar for about a week, but I dare you to make it last that long!

WHY
I DON'T EAT
AVOCADOS

I no longer buy or eat avocados on ethical grounds. The overconsumption and intensive production of avocados are having huge environmental and social impacts on the avocado-growing regions of Mexico, with permanent droughts, prices that are out of the reach of the local population and intensive farming methods that are poisoning the very soil they grow in.

STICKY HIBISCUS & CHIPOTLE SALSA

SERVES 4–6

This salsa is a celebration of all things tangy and spicy. I first came up with it after eating candied Korean chicken for the first time and falling in love with the textures and flavours of the dish. I immediately started playing with a Mexican version of it and this recipe is the result of about five years of testing. I hope you love it as much as I do. It's perfect with my chicken chicharrón tacos on page 32, but it's great for glazing and flavouring other meats too. You can make this sauce as hot or as mild as you want by increasing or reducing the amount of chipotles in adobo you use. Start with 60 grams, taste and adjust accordingly – remember, there is no way back with chillies!

FOR THE HIBISCUS INFUSION:

150ml water

30g dried hibiscus flowers

FOR THE SALSA:

50g caster sugar

10g garlic cloves, peeled

60ml agave syrup

50ml tequila

1 tbsp soy sauce

1 tbsp ketchup

60–80g chipotle chillies in adobo sauce, including some of the sauce

Start by making the hibiscus infusion. Combine the water and hibiscus flowers in a small heavy-based saucepan (I use a milk pan). Turn the heat up to high and as soon as the water begins to boil, switch the heat off, remove the pan from the heat and cover the pan with cling film – this is very important, as this will prevent any water from evaporating as it cools. Set aside for 15 minutes. As soon as the timer goes, tap the top of the cling film to make sure all the condensation accumulated on the plastic drops back into the infusion. Strain the infusion through a fine mesh sieve, pressing the hibiscus flowers well to extract as much of the ruby juice as possible.

Discard the used-up flowers and transfer the liquid to a blender or food processor with all the salsa ingredients and blend until smooth. Start by using 60g of chipotles to make this salsa medium-hot. Taste after blending and if it's not hot enough for you, add the rest of the chipotles in adobo before blending again.

Rinse the pan that you used to make the infusion (hibiscus always leaves grit and sediment on the bottom) and pour the blended sauce into it. Put the pan over a medium-high heat and bring the sauce to the boil. As soon as it starts boiling, lower the heat to medium-low and cook for 10–12 minutes, stirring regularly to prevent sticking, until the sauce is reduced by about half.

Lower the heat again – from here on out, it's all about reducing the sauce to get the right consistency. It should be thickish and sticky, a bit like runny honey (the sauce will thicken more once it starts cooling, so bear that in mind). It may take anything between 5 and 8 minutes more to get to the right consistency. Be patient during these last few minutes and stir constantly so the sauce doesn't burn or stick.

Once it's at the right consistency, remove the pan from the heat and set aside. If you're using the salsa later, leave it in the pan and reheat it gently just before you're going to use it. It keeps covered in the fridge for up to three weeks or you can freeze it.

SALSA MADURA

SERVES 4–6

This salsa recipe has been in my mother's family for a couple of generations. It was my late brother Pepillo's favourite salsa. My mam would make it with serrano chillies that were so over-ripe they were almost rotten (believe me, over-ripe chillies make the best version of this salsa) and it would be so hot, only he could eat it. A homemade jar of it was in his Christmas stocking every year. I've included it here as a little homage to his memory and his love for all things hot. Serrano chillies are hard to find in Ireland so you can use fresh red jalapeños, or for a milder version (which I recommend for the more sensitive Irish palate), red Kenyan chillies. Don't be afraid of the heat, this is absolutely delicious in small quantities.

235g fresh red jalapeño or Kenyan chillies, stemmed

1 litre water

50ml sunflower oil

1 large garlic clove, peeled

2½ tsp apple cider vinegar

1 tsp dried Mexican oregano

1 tsp flaky sea salt

Put the chillies and water in a medium-sized pot with a lid and bring to the boil, then lower the heat to medium. Let the chillies simmer, covered, for about 20 minutes. Drain the chillies and reserve about 50ml of the cooking water to use later. Shake any excess water off the chillies.

Transfer the chillies to a blender or food processor while they are still hot, along with the oil, whole garlic clove, vinegar, oregano, salt and one-third of the reserved cooking water. It's super important to blend this salsa while the chillies and liquid are still hot, as it helps to emulsify it to a creamy consistency. If you let the chillies or liquid go cold, the salsa won't work. Blend until you have a smooth, creamy salsa. If the salsa is very thick, add little bit more of the cooking liquid. It should have a loose but not overly runny consistency. Taste and correct the seasoning.

This salsa lasts in an airtight container with a lid for up to two weeks in the fridge.

Enjoy it with the roasted butternut squash tacos on page 42, as the tanginess and heat of this salsa complement that dish incredibly well.

SMOKY REFRIED BEANS

SERVES 4–6

Like most Mexicans, I absolutely adore beans and I couldn't fathom writing a book without a good recipe for them in it. Yet refried beans have an awful reputation. Most people think they're laden with fat, but in reality, they're quite the opposite. I much prefer to call them 'twice-cooked beans' since you cook them from raw and then pan-fry them in a little bit of oil. This is my cheat version, as not everybody has the patience for overnight soaking and 3 hours of careful simmering under a watchful eye. In fact, if you're asked out and you want to gently refuse the invitation, the equivalent of 'I'm washing my hair' in Mexico is 'I'm cooking beans'!

1 x 560g tin of whole black Mexican beans, drained (don't rinse them, as you don't want to wash away the flavour)

150ml water

2 chipotle chillies in adobo sauce

1 medium garlic clove, peeled

1 tsp dried Mexican oregano

½ tsp cumin seeds

½ tsp freshly ground black pepper

1 tbsp sunflower oil

80g finely diced onion

Put the drained beans in a blender or food processor with the water, chipotles, garlic, oregano, cumin seeds and pepper. Blend until you have a smooth sauce. Remember, you can make your refried beans hotter by adding extra chipotles or some of the delicious adobo sauce they come in. I always start with two chillies, blend and taste before adding more. There is no way back with chillies – once you have added too many, you can't take them out!

Heat the oil in a small non-stick frying pan on a medium-high heat. Add the onion and fry for 2 minutes, until translucent. Pour in the bean sauce, making sure to scrape all of it out. If you need to use a little bit of water to dislodge some of the beans, feel free to do so, just not too much (the more water you add, the longer you'll spend at the stove reducing the beans).

Lower the heat to medium and 'refry' your beans. Beans can stick to the bottom of the pan and burn quite quickly, so keep an eye on them. Cook for 12–15 minutes, stirring constantly, until they are the consistency of runny honey or custard. The beans will thicken more as they cool down, so bear that in mind. I tend to correct the seasoning at the end only if necessary, but most of the time I don't add any salt as the beans are already correctly seasoned in the tin.

TRY THIS

These beans are a great accompaniment to many Mexican dishes, but they are especially fab with the potato and chorizo tacos on page 28 and they are the star in the spicy bean and pan-roasted corn tacos on page 46.

MEXICAN SLAW

SERVES 4–6

This slaw is super fresh and tasty. In Mexico, it features in loads of taco toppings as it adds acidity and crunch and cuts through fatty meat fillings. The secret is to slice the cabbage as thinly as possible, almost like hair. Make sure you apply yourself to this job well – I promise it will make a difference.

½ small head of white cabbage

juice of 2 limes

1 small bunch of fresh coriander, leaves only

½ tsp flaky sea salt

Slice the cabbage as thinly as possible. I use a Japanese mandolin, but all food processors come with a thin slicing disc that will make the job super easy. If all else fails, take your time with a sharp knife.

Wash the cabbage well in a colander. If you're not eating your slaw within 20 minutes, leave the cabbage resting in a bowl of fresh cold water in the fridge to keep it crisp. Strain the cabbage about 20 minutes before you want to eat it and transfer it to a large bowl.

Pour the lime juice over the cabbage. Add the coriander leaves and season everything generously with flaky sea salt (I love Achill Island Smoked Sea Salt on this if you can get it).

Toss all the ingredients until well combined and let the slaw rest for 15 minutes before serving.

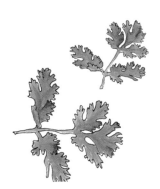

FRESH IS BEST

If you have any leftover slaw it will still be delicious the following day, but the longer you leave it, the more of a curtido (pickle) it will become. It will lose its crisp texture and the lime will start tasting old, so it's best to make it fresh on the day.

RED ONION PICKLE

SERVES 4–6

Hand on heart, this is the quickest and easiest pickle you'll ever make. It's traditionally served with pork pibil tacos (page 24) or any other pibil-style dishes. The acidity of the pickle combined with the sweetness of the onion cuts through the fattiness of the pork – it's a match made in heaven. If you are worried about heat, use only a quarter of a habanero chilli or leave it out altogether, it tastes good with or without it. This pickle is also delicious in cheese sandwiches or with a steak.

2 small red onions, peeled

½ small red habanero chilli (optional)

60ml extra virgin olive oil

60ml apple cider vinegar

¼ tsp dried Mexican oregano

½ tsp flaky sea salt

½ tsp freshly ground black pepper

Cut the onions in half lengthways from tip to root and slice them thinly, making sure every slice is the same thickness. Cutting the onion lengthways instead of around the 'equator' like you might usually do may feel a little unnatural, but if you are doing this by hand with a knife (as opposed to using a Japanese mandolin, like I do), you'll notice that it's easier to get slices that are a consistent thickness, which is of paramount importance for this recipe. If you have variations in thickness, you'll find that the slices pickle at different times so you will have some soft slices and some that are still crunchy. But every food processor comes with a slicing disc that will do all this for you.

Thinly slice the habanero chilli (if using), making sure to wash your hands well with plenty of cold water and soap both before and after touching the chilli. I don't bother deseeding the chilli (no self-respecting Mexican would!), but if it makes you feel better, go ahead and deseed it – just be warned that doing so doesn't get rid of the heat.

Boil your kettle and put the sliced onions and chilli in a medium-sized heatproof glass bowl (or something non-reactive). Pour the boiling water over the onions and chilli until they are all covered. Soak for 2–3 minutes – this partly cooks the onions and takes out some of their harshness. Set aside while you get the pickle going.

Combine the oil, vinegar, oregano, salt and pepper in a glass jug and mix with a small whisk or fork until well combined. Taste and check the seasoning – it should be sharp and well-seasoned, so add a little more salt and pepper if needed.

By now your onions should be almost translucent and the water should look a little cloudy. This is a sign that the onions are ready, so carefully strain the contents of the bowl, making sure to get rid of as much water as possible. Return the onions and chilli to the warm bowl – this is super important! Don't use a clean bowl. You need the same bowl that you soaked the onions in, as it's hot and that will help with the pickling.

Give the pickling liquid one final whisk and immediately pour it over the hot onions and chilli. The heat of the bowl and the heat of the onions will help the liquid to emulsify and it will kickstart the pickling process. Mix everything well with something non-reactive, like a rubber spatula or a wooden spoon, making sure everything is coated with the pickling liquid. My grandmother always warned us not to work with vinegar and metal utensils, as they may react chemically. A lot of the metals are now okay to use, but I keep the tradition just in case!

Set aside, uncovered, at room temperature for 1½–2 hours, stirring every half hour or so. As the onions pickle, you'll see them getting pinker and softer. I don't cover the bowl until its contents are completely cold. If you cover it while it's pickling, it might sweat and the condensation will drop back into the pickle, adding unnecessary moisture to the recipe, or worse, creating an environment where bacteria could grow.

If I have leftovers, which rarely happens, I store them covered with a cheesecloth or a thin tea towel in the coolest part of the kitchen (not in the fridge) for two days max. The fabric cover allows the pickle to breathe and prevents cross-contamination. I never bother bottling this pickle in sterilised jars as it's so easy to make a fresh batch and it tastes better.

PICO DE GALLO

SERVES 4–6

The first time I went to the cinema in Ireland, I ordered a hot dog and was handed a frankfurter in a bun with a packet of ketchup, some mustard and mayonnaise. I went looking for the pico de gallo bar, but there was none. Talk about culture shock! In Mexico, pico de gallo is a standard topping on hot dogs and every cinema has a station with all the fresh components of one so that you can finish your hot dog yourself. No pico de gallo? You can keep your hot dog, thank you very much! When I explained it to my husband, Alan, he cracked up laughing, but he eats hot dogs with pico de gallo now.

In Ireland, most people assume pico de gallo is a salsa, but I have been crushing that misconception in my classes for 15 years. It's a topping; at best you could call it a salsa cruda (raw sauce). I've allowed myself some creative licence with the addition of cucumber, which is not traditional at all and may the Aztec gods forgive me for it, but it's lovely with the fish tacos on page 38 – it adds freshness and sweetness to the overall dish and it makes me feel less predictable.

500g ripe tomatoes, finely diced

60g cucumber, finely diced

35g finely diced onion

1–2 fresh red jalapeño chillies, finely chopped

1 small bunch of fresh coriander, finely chopped

juice of 1 lime

a pinch of flaky sea salt

It takes no time to make this once everything is prepped ('Thank god after all that chopping!' I hear you say). Once everything is chopped, mix all the ingredients except the salt in a bowl and put it the fridge until you need it (but for no more than 30 minutes). I only season it right as I'm about to serve it because the salt will draw the moisture out of the tomatoes and will make the pico de gallo extremely juicy, which is not advisable if you want your taco to stay intact for as long as possible.

Pico de gallo is meant to be made fresh (no more than 30 minutes before you need it) if you want to avoid a soggy mess. It's much better eaten fresh anyway.

TRY THIS

Leftovers don't keep well, so blend them and cook them in a pan with a little bit of olive oil to be used as a salsa for eggs another day.

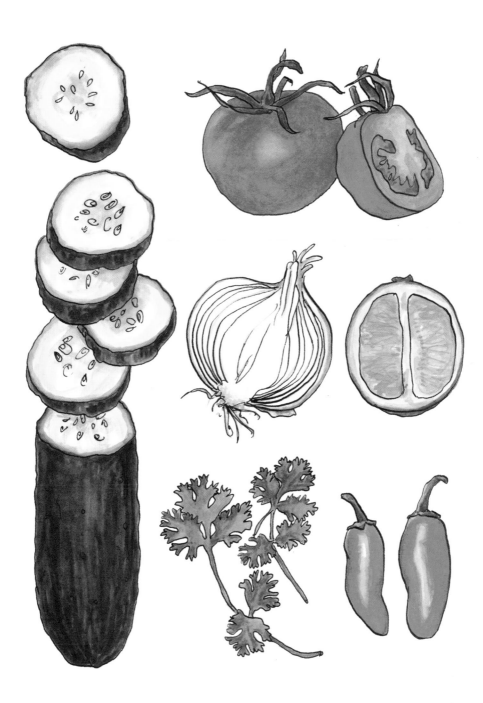

CITRUSY CREMA

SERVES 4–6

I came up with this recipe almost 20 years ago when I found my first chilli in Ireland and my other half needed a way to cope with heat in food. It's fresh, flavoursome and quick to make. The closest thing to Mexican crema is crème fraîche, so that's what I use. This is a staple at many of our supper clubs at Picado, as I find that having a bowl of this 'cooler' at the table makes people less nervous when they are eating hot salsas.

Don't make this more than a couple of hours in advance or the lime zest might become bitter. It's so quick and simple to make that you can easily make it on the day you need it. I particularly love it with my roasted butternut squash tacos on page 42, as the citrusy flavour of the crema balances out the bitterness of the ancho chilli and the sweetness of the squash, but we serve it with loads of other things too.

250g crème fraîche

2 tbsp full-fat milk

2 spring onions, thinly sliced

zest of 1 large lime

3 tbsp finely sliced fresh chives

flaky sea salt

TRY THIS

You can make a vegan version by using a good-quality vegan natural yogurt or a good vegan sour cream instead of the crème fraîche and a plant-based milk.

Pour the crème fraîche and milk into a medium-sized bowl and mix well to loosen and thin the crème fraîche.

Add the spring onions, lime zest, chives and a pinch of salt and gently incorporate everything with a spoon. Taste and correct the seasoning. Let it sit in the fridge for 1 hour or so to infuse the crème fraîche with all the flavours. Crème fraîche is a culture, so you might notice it has thickened when you take it out of the fridge to serve. Don't worry – just add 1 or 2 more tablespoons of milk and mix again to loosen it up. You want it to be the consistency of runny honey so that it can be drizzled over tacos.

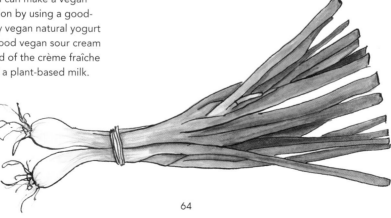

CHIPOTLE MAYONNAISE

SERVES 4–6

This is perhaps one of the easiest recipes to cheat in the entire Mexican repertoire. Most people will just buy a commercial mayonnaise and crush (or blend if they're fancy) some chipotles in adobo sauce into it. However, I love making mayonnaise from scratch. It always makes me feel so accomplished, plus it tastes so much better. Once you take out the fear of making mayonnaise, you can play around with the recipe and change the flavours and consistency as much as you like. The heat level is dictated by the chipotles in adobo, so if you want to make it hotter, add more chillies or add some of the thick adobo sauce that comes with them. The heat level in this one is medium-low.

3 chipotle chillies in adobo sauce

1 egg, at room temperature

juice of 1 lime

1 tsp flaky sea salt

1 tsp French's classic yellow mustard

200ml sunflower oil, in a measuring jug

Put the chipotles in a blender or food processor and blend for a couple of seconds to crush them. Add the egg, lime juice, salt and mustard and blend at low speed.

With the blender or food processor still running at low speed, start slowly adding the oil to the mixture, drop by drop, in a steady, continuous flow. Keep the machine going all the time and avoid pouring in the oil too quickly, as that can cause the mixture to split. Once you've used up all the oil, you will notice the mixture thickening and becoming a mayonnaise texture. Since I'm using this chipotle mayonnaise as a sauce to drizzle over my Ensenada-style fish tacos on page 38, I want it to have a relatively runny consistency.

Taste it and decide if you want to add a little bit more chilli to make it hotter. Once you're happy with it, transfer it to a serving bowl and chill in the fridge until you need it.

This mayonnaise keeps in the fridge for up to one week max. It has raw egg in it, so don't serve it to pregnant women or vegans (you can always do the cheat trick I mentioned in the intro for those cases where raw egg is a problem).

INDEX

Nine Bean Rows Books

23 Mountjoy Square

Dublin 1, Ireland

@9beanrowsbooks

ninebeanrowsbooks.com

NINE
BEAN
ROWS

Blasta Books is an imprint of Nine Bean Rows Books Ltd.

@blastabooks blastabooks.com

First published 2022

Copyright © Lily Ramirez-Foran, 2022

ISBN: 978-1-9993799-0-2

Editor: Kristin Jensen

Series artist: Nicky Hooper
nickyhooper.com

Designer: Jane Matthews
janematthewsdesign.com

Proofreader: Jocelyn Doyle

Printed by L&C Printing Group, Poland

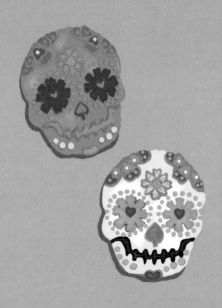